ENDANGERED!

EAGLES

Casey Horton

Series Consultant: James G. Doherty
General Curator, The Bronx Zoo, New York

BENCHMARK BOOKS

MARSHALL CAVENDISH
NEW YORK

Benchmark Books
Marshall Cavendish Corporation
99 White Plains Road
Tarrytown, New York 10591-9001

Library of Congress Cataloging-in-Publication Data

Horton, Casey.
   Eagles / Casey Horton.
     p.   cm. — (Endangered!)
   Includes bibliographical references (p.   ) and index.
   ISBN 0-7614-0214-4
   1. Eagles—Juvenile literature.   2. Endangered species—Juvenile literature.   [1. Eagles. 2. Endangered species.]   I. Title.
II. Series: Horton, Casey. Endangered!
QL696.F32H67 1995
598.9'16—dc20   95-12426
                                             CIP
                                           AC

Printed in Hong Kong

PICTURE CREDITS

The publishers would like to thank the following picture libraries for supplying the photographs used in this book: Ardea 19; Frank Lane Picture Agency FC, 2, 4, 5, 6, 7, 8, 9, 10, 11, 13, 14, 15, 20, 21, 22, 24, 26, 27, 28, BC; Frank Lane Picture Agency/Silvestris 18, 29; Natural History Photographic Agency 25; Survival Anglia 16, 17.

Series created by Brown Packaging

Front cover: Bald eagle.
Title page: White-tailed eagle.
Back cover: Bald eagle.

Contents

Introduction

The imperial eagle is a wonderful hunter, but it cannot cope with the changes that people are making in the areas where it lives.

Eagles are among the supreme hunters of the bird world. Some kinds feed mainly on fish. Others specialize in eating snakes. Then there are those that hunt mainly small or medium-sized **mammals**.

All eagles are wonderfully well equipped for hunting. They have fantastic eyesight for spotting **prey**, sharp claws for grasping their victims, and downward-curving bills for tearing flesh. They are also powerful fliers. Yet, of the more than 50 kinds of eagles in the world today, many are in danger of becoming **extinct**.

During the millions of years that birds have lived on Earth, there have been many natural changes in the environment. Some birds were unable to **adapt** to them, and so became extinct. Others, though, became accustomed to these changes and survived.

Today people are making many changes to the environment. They are cutting down forests where the birds live, for example. The problem is that now the birds have no chance to adapt to these changes, because they are happening too quickly. As a result, many different kinds of birds are in danger of vanishing from the planet forever.

In this book we will look at eight kinds of eagles that are at risk. We will start with the bald eagle, the national bird of the United States.

A white-tailed eagle feeds its young at its nest on a rocky ledge. Although it is protected by law, the white-tailed eagle is in danger of dying out.

Areas where the bald eagle can be found

The mighty bald eagle can catch and eat fish up to a foot (30 cm) long.

Bald Eagle

The bald eagle is mainly brown in color, but it has a striking white head and neck, and a white tail. It is a large eagle, measuring 2 ft 6 in-3 ft 7 in (76-110 cm) long and weighing up to 16½ lb (7.5 kg).

The bald eagle lives only in North America and can be found in most parts of the continent. It eats mainly fish and makes its home near rivers and lakes and on the coast.

One of the bald eagle's favorite foods is salmon. It usually hunts these fish by watching from a perch overlooking a river. When it spies a fish moving in the water, the eagle takes off and swoops low over the surface, snatching up the fish with its claws. The bird then flies off to a perch, where it eats its catch.

Besides fish, the bald eagle eats waterbirds, such as ducks. It has two ways of catching them. Sometimes it circles at a great height over the water, chooses a victim from among the birds below, and then drops down on it at enormous speed. At other times, the eagle surprises its prey by flying in low over the water, hiding behind the waves.

A bald eagle reaches down with its claws as it prepares to snatch a fish from just below the surface of the water.

Bald Eagle

The bald eagle was once common throughout much of North America, but then its numbers fell. The bird even disappeared from parts of its **range**. Many bald eagles suffered as a result of poisoning. For years, farmers and ranchers left out poisoned bait to kill animals they regarded as pests, which included the bald eagle. Sometimes eagles died directly from eating the bait. Often, though, the poison got into the water, poisoning the fish. There was normally not enough poison in these fish to kill the eagles outright.

Four bald eagles perch on a branch. The second from the left is a young bird. Only adults have the pure white head and tail.

However, there was enough to cause female eagles to lay eggs with shells that were too thin. When they tried to **incubate** their eggs, the shells broke. In this way, the birds were stopped from producing young, and numbers fell.

The bald eagle was also put at risk by hunting. Ranchers shot bald eagles because they believed they attacked their young cattle and sheep. Fishermen hunted the eagles because they thought the birds took too many fish. In fact, the United States government used to pay fishermen in Alaska for each bald eagle they killed.

Now it is against the law to hunt the bald eagle or to use chemicals that might harm it. As a result, numbers are increasing, and the bald eagle has started to return to areas in which it had died out. Though the bird is not yet fully out of danger, its future now looks much brighter.

A bald eagle flies low over water in Alaska. Thousands of bald eagles were killed in Alaska before the bird was protected there. Now, more bald eagles live in Alaska than anywhere else.

The white-tailed eagle is the largest eagle in Europe.

White-tailed Eagle

The white-tailed eagle is a large, heavy eagle, measuring 2 ft 3 in-3 ft 1 in (68-94 cm) in length. It is mainly brown in color, with a lighter-colored head and a short, white, wedge-shaped tail. Its wings are broad and long. They span more than 6 ft 6 in (2 m) when outstretched.

The white-tailed eagle lives in many parts of Europe and Asia. It is most at home along rocky coasts. For this reason, it is sometimes called the white-tailed sea eagle, though it can be found inland along river valleys and near lakes.

The diet of the white-tailed eagle includes fish, birds, mammals, and a large amount of **carrion** (dead animal flesh). The bird often hunts by soaring on outstretched wings, watching the ground below, or by flying low over water, hoping to surprise an unwary seabird. It also searches for prey by sitting on a perch and scanning the surrounding countryside. This is known as **still hunting**. As we have seen, bald eagles also often hunt in this way.

A young white-tailed eagle flies overhead. When they soar, white-tailed eagles can look like vultures.

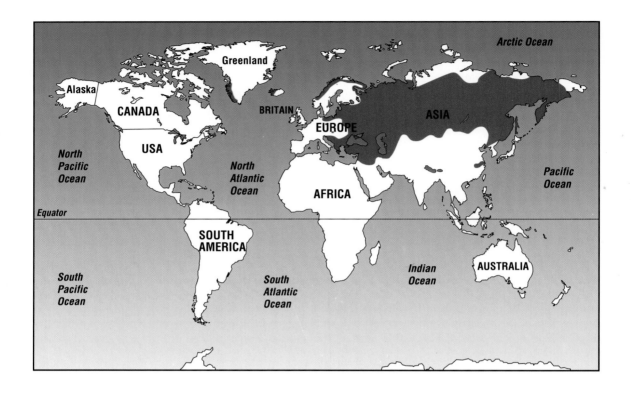

The white-tailed eagle is particularly fond of eating sea ducks, which gather in flocks on open water. An eagle chooses a single duck from among the flock. Then it flies at the bird, attacking it again and again, until the victim is too weak to dive or fly away. The eagle then plucks its exhausted prey from the water and carries it off.

There are now far fewer white-tailed eagles than there were, especially in Europe. In fact, in parts of its range, the eagle has become extinct. White-tailed eagles have been shot by farmers who thought the birds killed their animals. They have also died from eating food poisoned by **pollution** and from poisoned bait left out by farmers to kill

Areas where the white-tailed eagle can be found

other animals. The white-tailed eagle is now protected by law in most places in which it lives. But it is hard to make sure people obey the law.

There is some good news, however. In Britain, the white-tailed eagle had become extinct by the early 1900s. Then, in 1976, **conservationists** brought some white-tailed eagles from Norway to northern Britain. They released them into the wild on an island set aside as a **reserve**. The birds settled in, and today there are once again white-tailed eagles soaring across British skies.

A white-tailed eagle with its prey. Besides fish and waterbirds, white-tailed eagles eat small mammals, such as rabbits.

RUSSIA

CHINA

JAPAN

Pacific Ocean

Areas where Steller's sea eagle can be found in summer

Steller's sea eagle shows off its huge orange bill.

Steller's Sea Eagle

Steller's sea eagle is one of the most magnificent of all the **birds of prey**. Most of its plumage (coat of feathers) is dark brown, but it has pure white shoulders, legs, and tail feathers. Steller's sea eagle is large, too. It measures 2 ft 11 in-3 ft 4 in (89-102 cm) in length, and some birds weigh more than 20 lb (9 kg).

Fish is Steller's main food, but no animal up to the size of an arctic fox or a goose is safe from this mighty bird. Carrion is also eaten. Indeed, this bird even visits slaughterhouses to feed on the remains of dead animals. During the warmer months, Steller's sea eagle is found along the Pacific coast of Russia. When the weather gets colder, however, and food there becomes hard to find, many birds **migrate** elsewhere. A large number spend the winter on the northern Japanese island of Hokkaido.

Steller's sea eagle is rare, but scientists do not believe that it is in danger of dying out at present. The bird seems to be safe during the summer because it lives a long way from people. However, in winter it makes its home closer to where people live. This increases the danger of the bird's being poisoned by pollution in the waters that it fishes, or of its being shot as a pest. This may explain the fall in the number of Steller's sea eagles.

The wings of a Steller's sea eagle can measure over 8 ft (2.5 m) from tip to tip, when the bird is in flight.

Areas where Pallas's fish eagle can be found

Pallas's fish eagle belongs to a group of medium-sized fish eagles that also includes the African and Madagascar fish eagles.

Pallas's Fish Eagle

Pallas's fish eagle is less colorfully marked than some of the other fish eagles, but it is still a handsome bird. It is mostly dark brown, but its head, neck, and throat are light in color, and its brown tail has a broad white band. Pallas's

measures 2 ft 3 in-2 ft 6 in (69-75 cm) in length and is more lightly built than the eagles we have covered so far.

Pallas's fish eagle is sometimes called Pallas's sea eagle. But it is rarely found along the coast and usually makes its home near rivers and swamps in central Asia, China, and northern India. Because the eagles are scattered over such a large area, it is difficult for scientists to study them. However, Pallas's fish eagle is considered to be at risk and numbers have fallen in some parts of its range. Chemical pollution of the water in which the birds fish is thought to be one cause.

The diet of Pallas's fish eagle includes waterbirds. This eagle is feeding on a duck.

AFRICA

Equator

Atlantic
Ocean

MADAGASCAR

Indian Ocean

Area where the
Madagascar fish
eagle can be found

*Madagascar
fish eagles
build a large
nest of sticks
at the top of a
tall tree.*

Madagascar Fish Eagle

This eagle lives only on the island of Madagascar, which
lies off the east coast of Africa. The bird is mainly brown,
with white cheeks and tail, and with rust-colored streaks on
its chest and head. It is 23-25 in (58-64 cm) long.

The Madagascar fish eagle makes its home mostly in
forests near lakes and rivers, though it can also be found in

swamps and along rocky coasts. It feeds mainly on fish and crabs, and eats little carrion.

This eagle is one of the rarest birds of prey. People have drained swamps and cleared forests to make way for crops, so the bird has lost much of its **habitat**. To make matters worse, mining work has muddied Madagascar's rivers. As a result, fewer fish can live in the rivers and the eagles have trouble spotting them in the cloudy water.

Only around 100 of these eagles remain. Some live in Madagascar's reserves and national parks. New protected areas for the eagles are being planned, though.

A close relative of the Madagascar fish eagle is the African fish eagle (pictured here). It is threatened by pollution in some parts of Africa.

Bay of
Bengal

SOUTHEAST
ASIA

Andaman
Islands

Indian
Ocean

North
China
Sea

*Area where the
Andaman snake
eagle can be found*

*The Andaman
snake eagle is
also known as
the dark snake
eagle.*

Andaman Snake Eagle

The Andaman snake eagle is around 22 in (56 cm) long
and is dark brown with light-colored spots on its chest and
belly. It is found only on the Andaman Islands in the Bay
of Bengal, where it makes its home in forest clearings.

Snake eagles get their name from the fact that they feed
mainly on snakes. They have much thicker claws than

other eagles. With these, the birds can crush their prey to death quickly, before it can bite. This is important, since the eagles can be killed by snake poison.

Scientists know very little about the life of the Andaman snake eagle. But they do know that it is a very rare bird of prey that cannot survive outside the forests of the Andaman Islands. These are its only home, and if they disappear, so will the eagle. One of the islands' products is hardwood timber, and many forests have already been cut down to supply this. They have been replaced with rubber plantations and rice fields. At the moment, though, enough forests remain so that the Andaman snake eagle is not in immediate danger of extinction. But it is far from safe.

An Andaman snake eagle takes to the air from its perch in a tree.

The imperial eagle is a fine-looking bird. Because of this, many imperials have been captured alive for sale to collectors.

Imperial Eagle

Imperial eagles are large, powerful eagles that live in parts of Europe and Asia. Once they could also be found in some areas of North Africa. They are blackish-brown with yellowish feathers on the top of the head and the back of the neck, and some white on the shoulders. They are 2 ft 7 in-2 ft 9 in (79-84 cm) long and weigh 7-9 lb (3.1-4 kg), though imperials that live in Spain and Portugal are a little smaller. They also look slightly different, having more white on the shoulders.

Though they also eat carrion, snakes, and birds, imperial eagles feed mainly on mammals. The Spanish and Portuguese birds are particularly fond of rabbits and hares. Ground squirrels are the imperial's favorite food elsewhere in its range. Imperials need about 14-21 oz (400-600 g) of food a day. Like other big eagles, they are usually "still hunters," though they are good fliers when they need to be.

Imperials are lowland eagles that like to live in areas containing a mixture of grassland and trees. This has often brought them into contact with people. It seems that in general, imperials simply cannot put up with living side by side with people. Often, when settlers move into an area,

Areas where the imperial eagle can be found

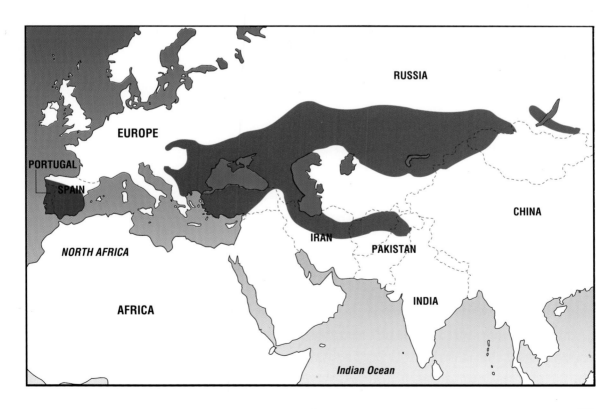

The imperial eagle has legs that are feathered down to their feet. For this reason, it is known as a "booted" eagle.

the eagles move out. This, like habitat destruction, results in too many eagles being crowded into too small a space. Meanwhile, many of those that have remained near human settlements have been shot as pests and harmed by farm chemicals. They have also died from eating poisoned bait left out for other animals. On top of that, many have been killed by accidentally crashing into electrical power lines. Scientists think that only a few thousand imperials are left, and these are widely scattered throughout their range.

The Spanish and Portuguese eagles are in the worst trouble – perhaps only 200-300 remain. Like other imperials, they have been hunted. Also, people have robbed their nests of eggs. These eagles are protected by law, but it is hard to make sure that people obey the law. Some people continue to hunt the birds and rob their nests.

The main problem facing imperial eagles in Spain and Portugal, however, is that they have hardly anywhere left to live. People have turned nearly all of their habitat into farmland. One place in which the birds can live safely is the Doñana National Park, in southern Spain. The number of eagles living there has steadily increased. Unfortunately, one reserve cannot provide food for many eagles. These large birds need more reserves if they are to survive.

Spanish and Portuguese imperials differ slightly from other imperial eagles and are sometimes known as Adalbert's eagles.

Areas where the
Philippine eagle
can be found

*The Philippine
eagle used to
be known as
the monkey-
eating eagle.*

Philippine Eagle

The Philippine eagle is an enormously powerful bird of
prey that lives only on the Philippine Islands in the Pacific.
It has a brown back, is white underneath, and its bill is
heavy and dark, with a fiercely hooked tip. A crest of
feathers on the head adds to the bird's striking appearance.
Female Philippine eagles can weigh up to 15½ lb (7 kg)
and measure almost 3 ft (90 cm) in length. Male eagles are
a little smaller.

   The Philippine eagle makes its home in **rainforests**. Its
coloration helps it blend in with the trees so that it can sit

and watch for prey without being seen. The Philippine eagle feeds on monkeys and other medium-sized mammals, but it also eats snakes and large birds.

The Philippine eagle is in serious danger of becoming extinct. This is mainly because the bird's rainforest home is being cut down for timber. Not only is the Philippine eagle losing more and more of its home each day, but roads – built to move the timber – are making it easier for hunters to enter the forest. Because of their handsome appearance, Philippine eagles have long been hunted, often to be stuffed and sold to tourists.

The Philippine eagle has exceptionally strong feet with needle-sharp claws.

The Philippine government has made the Philippine eagle the national bird so that people will be proud of it and stop killing it.

The Philippine government is trying hard to protect the eagle. It has made hunting the bird illegal and is trying to control the cutting down of trees. But it is difficult to stop people from breaking these laws. Unless the Philippine rainforest is saved, the eagle will become extinct in the wild. Since no one has yet bred a Philippine eagle in **captivity**, this magnificent bird of prey could soon disappear forever.

As we have seen, the Philippine eagle is not the only bird that is losing its forest home. All over the world, trees are being cut down in great numbers. This is unlikely to stop immediately. Many of the countries concerned are poor, and selling timber is a way of making money. Also, people in these places need land on which to live. One answer is to set aside large areas of forest as permanent reserves. If we can do this – and keep hunting and pollution under control – then eagles will continue to soar in the skies of the future.

The most powerful eagle in the world is the harpy eagle (left). It was believed to be seriously endangered, but recent studies have brought good news. There are more harpies than scientists thought, so the bird has been taken off the danger list.

Useful Addresses

For more information about eagles and how you can help protect them, contact these organizations:

Hawk Mountain Sanctuary Association
Route 2
Box 191
Kempton, PA 19529

National Audubon Society
950 Third Avenue
New York, N.Y. 10022

National Wildlife Federation
1400 16th Street NW
Washington, D.C. 20036

U.S. Fish and Wildlife Service
Endangered Species and Habitat
Conservation
400 Arlington Square
18th and C Streets NW
Washington, D.C. 20240

World Wildlife Fund
1250 24th Street NW
Washington, D.C. 20037

World Wildlife Fund Canada
90 Eglinton Avenue East
Suite 504
Toronto
Ontario M4P 2Z7

Further Reading

The Bird Atlas Barbara Taylor (New York: Dorling Kindersley, 1993)

Birds of Prey Norman Barrett (New York: Franklin Watts, 1991)

Endangered Wildlife of the World (New York: Marshall Cavendish Corporation, 1993)

Extinct Birds: And Those in Danger of Extinction Philip Steele (New York: Franklin Watts, 1991)

Saving Endangered Birds: Ensuring a Future in the Wild Thane Maynard (New York: Franklin Watts, 1993)

Vanishing Eagles Philip Burton (New York: Dodd, Mead, 1983)

Where the Bald Eagles Gather Dorothy Hinshaw Patent (New York: Clarion, 1984)

Wildlife of the World (New York: Marshall Cavendish Corporation, 1994)

Glossary

Adapt: To change in order to survive in new conditions.

Bird of prey: A type of bird with a hooked bill and clawed feet that hunts and eats other animals.

Captivity: Confinement; for animals, usually in a cage.

Carrion (KAR-ee-uhn): Dead animal flesh.

Conservationist (Kon-ser-VAY-shun-ist): A person who protects and preserves the Earth's natural resources, such as animals, plants, and soil.

Extinct (Ex-TINKT): No longer living anywhere in the world.

Habitat: The place where an animal lives. For example, the Andaman snake eagle's habitat is the forest.

Incubate (IN-kyew-bait): In birds, to sit on eggs in order to keep them warm so they will hatch.

Mammal: A kind of animal that is warm-blooded and has a backbone. Most are covered with fur or have hair. Females have glands that produce milk to feed their young.

Migrate: To move from one place to another to live. Many birds leave their homes before winter to migrate to warmer places. They return home in summer.

Pollution (Puh-LOO-shun): Materials, such as garbage, fumes, and chemicals, that damage the environment.

Prey: An animal that is hunted and eaten by another animal.

Rainforest: A forest that has heavy rainfall much of the year.

Range: The area in the world in which a particular kind of animal can be found.

Reserve: Land that has been set aside for plants and animals to live in without being harmed.

Still hunting: A method of hunting used by large birds of prey. The bird sits still on a perch, watching for a victim. When it spots one, it swoops down and catches it.

Index